David Taylor, the well-known wildlife vet and regular guest on BBC television's *Animal Magic*, gives specialist, helpful and humorous advice on living with and caring for your dog. Everything the dog lover needs to know is presented with the aid of diagrams and some light-hearted cartoons.

In the same series
THE CAT

In preparation
THE PONY
THE SMALL PET
THE CAGE-BIRD
THE EXOTIC PET

Also by the same author
ZOOVET: THE WORLD OF A WILDLIFE VET
DOCTOR IN THE ZOO
GOING WILD: MORE ADVENTURES OF A ZOO VET

THE DOG

An Owner's Maintenance Manual

DAVID TAYLOR, FRCVS

London
UNWIN PAPERBACKS
Boston   Sydney

First published in Unwin Paperbacks 1980

UNWIN® PAPERBACKS
40 Museum Street, London WC1A 1LU

© David Taylor, 1980

British Library Cataloguing in Publication Data

Taylor, David, *b.1934*
  The dog.
  1. Dogs
  I. Title
  636.7'08'3   SF427   79-41539

  ISBN 0-04-636012-3

Typeset in 10 on 11 point Times,
and printed in Great Britain by
Hunt Barnard Printing Ltd., Aylesbury, Bucks

Contents

The common phrase, 'going to the dogs', originates from the game of dice in ancient Rome where the 'one' was called canis *(dog). Throwing three 'ones' lost everything, and thus 'dog' meant ruin and 'going to the dogs' a spell of bad luck.*

Introduction

What is a dog? According to the dictionary it can be the male of a species; a cowardly, worthless, surly fellow; the name of two constellations of stars; a mechanical device for gripping or holding; one of a pair of irons for supporting burning wood in a fireplace; short for dog-fish; an old West Indian copper or silver coin; an abbreviation of the nautical dog-watch; a verb meaning to follow closely or to have sexual connection with on all fours; a corruption by reversal of the word 'God' in colloquial oaths; and a slang term for the lowly sausage. It is all of these and more.

The more is what this book is concerned with: a quadruped of the genus *Canis, Canis familiaris*, the domestic dog.

Now the most popular domestic pet (though being strongly challenged by the cat, which has within the past few years pushed the budgerigar into third place), the dog holds a powerful and quite unique position in human society. It is the ripened relationship of two more or less carnivorous animals that have rubbed shoulders, shared house, food, weather and fortune, exploited, quarrelled with and fawned over one another, laboured and endured together for a hundred centuries. Not even the horse, and certainly not the budgerigar or cat, has been so intimately involved in man's recent evolution. Man has employed dogs in a rich variety of ways – as guards, hunters, war-machines, seeing-eyes, rodent controllers, draught animals, foot-warmers and providers of hair and meat.

Mastiffs in light armour, carrying spikes and cauldrons of flaming sulphur and resin on their backs, were used in warfare by the Romans and in the Middle Ages, particularly against mounted knights. Sadly updated, dogs were trained by the Russians in the last war to carry out suicide missions against German tanks. They would run between the tracks of the vehicles with mines strapped to their backs. The mine would explode as soon as a vertical antenna attached to it touched the metal of the tank.

Carts pulled by dogs were used in Belgium, Holland, Germany and Switzerland until quite recently. Such canine labour was forbidden by law in Great Britain in 1885. Now a 'dog cart' refers to a light, pony-drawn carriage with a box underneath for carrying the dogs in restful style.

Dogs are still eaten by man in Asia, where red-coloured specimens are for some reason particularly prized. The Chinese consumed considerable numbers of chow-chows and other red dogs until recently. The Aztecs of Mexico, apart from depending on dog hair to make cloth (they had no cotton or wool), also fattened a non-barking, hairless breed of dog for the table. These poor creatures were the only source of domestic meat apart from the turkey. 'Sad-faced and uncomplaining – even when. beaten,' Father Clavigero, a Spanish missionary, described them. For canine gastronomes the most famous town in Mexico was Acolman, where edible dogs of great delicacy were raised on bread, green corn, meat and food that had gone bad.

Australian aborigines use dingoes for warmth on cold nights by sleeping with them clasped in their arms. Women, when not carrying young children, often 'wear' a dog draped across the lower back with the head and tail in the crook of their arms as a kidney-warmer. So much for red flannel!

The peoples of Mesopotamia used giant mastiffs to hunt lions, while the Jews shunned all contact with what they regarded as an unclean, dung-heap-frequenting beast: it is interesting that some biblical scholars interpret the passage in St Mark's Gospel (chapter 7, verses 24–30) where a foreign (non-Jewish) woman sought help from Christ, as indicating that she actually had a pet dog with her.

The poor old dog was even used in times gone by to harvest the most magical of plants. The mandrake, or mandragora, was the source of a coveted narcotic and aphrodisiac extract. The snag was that the mandrake, whose split root often presents the two-legged appearance of a manikin, could not be pulled from the earth without producing fatal effects on the puller, or so primitive people believed. So one end of a cord was attached to the root and the other was tied round a dog's neck. The theory was that when the dog was chased away, out would come the wondrous root (often with a terrible shriek, it was said) and down would drop the luckless mutt, dead as a doornail.

In every age across the globe, it seems, folk have in one way or another echoed the words of St Bernard (*c.* AD 1150), 'Who loves me will love my dog also', yet by some oversight, dogs do not normally come supplied with their own maintenance manual. But what appears to be good for the family motor-car, the dumb and relatively simple *Automobilus horrendus*, must surely be even more so for best friend, *Canis*.

What follows is concerned with practical matters, the maintenance and servicing of the Family Dog by common or garden doting owners. I am not concerned with expert breeders or the show-bench fraternity but solely with those running or being run by a mutt for all of a thousand different reasons, and particularly with L-drivers about to be taken to the park by their first pup.

Around $5\frac{1}{2}$ million dogs are kept as pets in Great Britain and at least 50 million in the USA. There are over a hundred breeds. Although their sizes and shapes vary enormously, all dogs are essentially the same design of animal, not far removed from their primitive ancestors. They are highly adaptable creatures, and the process of evolution hasn't found it necessary to alter them much. They are a resilient species capable of providing abundant human happiness – if treated with a modicum of intelligence. With any luck, fifteen, sixteen or even more years of healthy life lie ahead of Fido as he drowses with your foot as his pillow and his tummy comfortably full of marrow-bone jelly. This little book is designed for the dog's faithful companion and friend, you, so that you can make the most of him. If you're ready, then, let's go to the dogs!

1

The phrase, 'the hair of the dog that bit you', refers to the ancient notion that the burnt hair of a dog is an antidote to its bite. An alternative cure was to be obtained by use of the dog's liver. As recently as 1866 it was stated at an inquest in the north of England that after a child had been bitten, the dog was killed and thrown into a river. It was subsequently pulled out so that part of its liver could be extracted, cooked and given to the child. Despite this remedy, which many witnesses considered fool-proof, the infant died.

This Year's Models

What's that lying on your hearth rug? Could it really be a Loewchen, an Akita, a Bichon frise or a Glen of Imaal? No, they're not the names of fashionable painters or brands of scotch malt, but dogs. True, such exotic mutts are so uncommon that I doubt whether one in a thousand of us could recognise them if they leapt into our arms or gnawed at our ankles. As for a Sharkskin or a Caes de Agua, even rarer breeds with barely two dozen of the former and only twice as many of the latter dotted round this planet, I'll bet my bottom dollar that the untidy pile sprawled there, hogging the fire glow and twitching and baying softly as he pursues next door's cat across his dreams, isn't one of those. And it really doesn't matter. Blue-blooded or of doubtful parentage, ten ounce chihuahua or fifteen-stone St Bernard, he or she is special, one of a resourceful species that has been around man for over ten thousand years.

About forty million years ago, a small, weasel-like mammal with a well developed brain for its size climbed through the trees of the Eocene period. Its name was *Miacis* and it was the forefather of the group of living animals that we call Canids, the dog, wolf and fox family. The family tree is shown below.

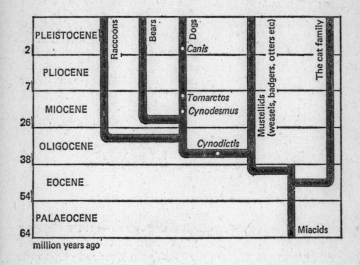

million years ago

Dogs as we know them first came on the scene in Eurasia between twelve and fourteen thousand years ago. From what kind of animal did they directly spring? The old idea that it was a form of jackal or jackal/wolf cross has been abandoned. Now we believe it was the smaller southern strain of the grey wolf, to be found in China and India. At the time the grey wolf, an animal with a wide variety of coat colours, was distributed throughout Europe, Asia and North America.

The suggestion that breeds such as the chihuahua sprang from crossing between dogs and rabbits or rodents, though widely believed, is completely false, as of course is the even more outlandish claim that creatures half-dog and half-human can occur. Statements to this effect by such illustrious medical men of days gone by as Ambroise Paré, who described and sketched a 'dog-boy' born in 1493, are now known to refer to rare congenital deformities or tumours. There are accounts of men with dogs' heads in many civilisations. Marco Polo said that these people lived on the

Paré's 'dog boy'

Andaman Islands in the Indian Ocean. Perhaps the mediaeval Sir John Mandeville, who wrote of dog-men inhabiting an island called Macumera, was referring to the same place. If so, the origins of the fable lie in the first sightings of dog-faced baboons. Another animal which may have misled our forefathers was the indris, a large lemur of Madagascar with a dog-like head and a very human-like body. In Byzantine art, St Christopher is often depicted with a canine head. This possibly represents the assimilation into Christianity of

Miacis – the first dog

the old Egyptian dog-headed god, Anubis, though there is also the legend that the saint was so uncommonly handsome that he prayed for God to give him a dog's head to stop the girls pursuing him.

Indris – the 'dog man'!

The domestic dog spread rapidly all over the world except for Australia. Some scientists believe that the process of domestication began first with wild dogs scavenging in the middens of human habitations. Others think that the first contact between humans and dogs was when early man hunted dogs for food, killed the adults and took litters of puppies back to the homestead for fattening up.

By the Bronze Age, four distinct types of dog can be recognised from fossil remains:

1   Wolf-like (similar to the Eskimo dog of today)
2   Sheepdog
3   Various hounds
4   Small house-dogs

When the first Europeans arrived in North and South America, they found at least twenty distinct dog breeds; now the Mexican hairless and the Eskimo dogs are the only surviving native breeds. One of the ancient native breeds of African dogs is the basenji, and equally venerable Middle Eastern breeds are the saluki and the Kurdish herding dog. The dingo is not native to Australia but was introduced thousands of years ago by the first immigrants. Wherever they spread, dogs thrived because of their moderate specialisation, adaptability, high intelligence and use of social co-operation (the power of the pack). Whereas the lone cat relies on stalking skills, the gregarious dog makes hunting a group activity with emphasis on un-cat-like tenacity and stamina.

If you've already got your heart on a beagle or a basenji, anything I say won't change your mind. But if it is good nature and docility that you want, and you don't require a hell-hound to patrol your mansion at night, dismembering intruders in the process, this list will be of some interest:

The top five breeds of dog least likely to bite
1   Labrador retriever
2   Golden retriever   4   Old English sheepdog
3   Shetland sheepdog   5   Yorkshire terrier

Runners-up are the Welsh terrier, beagle, dalmatian and pointer.

However, should you need that hell-hound to protect the family silver, here is another list:

The top five breeds of dog most likely to bite
1 Alsatian
2 Chow
3 Poodle
4 Fox terrier
5 Italian bulldog

Runners-up are the airedale and pekingese – with the Dobermann pinscher nowhere in sight! Incidentally, there are more dog bites in June than in any other month.

There is an ever-changing 'top of the pops' in dog owners' tastes. As with cars, the pattern of makes to be seen roaming the highways and byways gradually shifts. A breed comes 'in', like beagles and poodles in recent years. Others become somewhat passé, as have fox terriers and bulldogs. Luckily the dog doesn't have the built-in obsolescence of most makes of automobile. On the other hand, the scurvy brigade of owners who swell the numbers of animals being euthanased at animal clinics just before summer holidays and just after Christmas are surely more callous than folk who purchase old bangers for next to nothing in the hope of one good, final run.

So, if you like to go with the crowd, here are the most popular breeds at the moment according to registrations made at the Kennel Club:

1   Yorkshire terrier
2   Alsatian
3   Labrador retriever
4   Cocker spaniel
5   Rough collie

My favourite? The first pup you come across in the kennels of the local humane society clinic. That's how I got the finest dog one could find – a mongrel bitch pup in need of a home before its ten days in Death Row were up.

2

He is not certain whether he did not twice a week, for twenty years, taste dog's nose, which your committee find, upon inquiry, to be compounded of warm porter, moist sugar, gin and nutmeg.

Charles Dickens: *Pickwick Papers*

Specifications

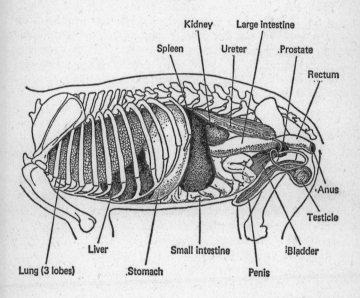

The dog is essentially an animal of the chase: enduring, patient, intelligent and fleet of foot. He is a fine digger and characteristically 'marks' his territory, whether it be sun-dappled African savannah or five square yards of rain-swept back yard, with urine to stake his claim most eloquently and clearly to his fellows if a trifle smellily to human beings. He instinctively covers his droppings with dirt, although in the domestic animal this behaviour has often degenerated into merely scratching theatrically with the hind feet in the general vicinity of the droppings. Most of all he is a sociable beast, with none of the aloof, lordly go-it-alone of the cat family. This is clearly seen in packs of wild dogs, where group ambushes are cleverly set up and un-attached adults are recruited as baby sitters for pups while parents go a-hunting.

The dog family, which includes foxes, jackals and wolves (but excludes the Tasmanian wolf, which is a pouch-carrying marsupial of dog-like appearance), is not highly specialised biologically. In fact, its broad adaptability and multi-purpose form have been prime factors in its survival world-wide. Nevertheless, it is important to consider some of the dog's systems which contribute to the animal's ability to survive and which are generally common to dingo and dachshund, Cape hunting dog and cocker spaniel.

SPEED

Every schoolboy knows that the cheetah is the world's fastest land mammal, achieving speeds of 63 mph and possibly up to 80 mph over short distances. Some antelope have been clocked at 61 mph, but again only for relatively short distances (approximately 200 yards). But hunting in the animal world is often carried out over long distances. An antelope that made an initial burst of 60 mph will soon be forced to drop to 30 mph or less as its energy drains away. Here is where the persistent, long-distance runners of the dog family come into their own. Cape (African) hunting dogs will pace one another, some loping behind for a while as others race ahead. When the leaders tire, the lopers move to the front and keep up the relentless pace of the vanguard. After a long chase this species will actually run down and kill lions.

Wolves can achieve speeds of around 35 mph, greyhounds have been recorded at 41·72 mph and the saluki is thought to touch 43 mph.

A quick mover of a slightly different sort must have been Jenny Lind, a bull terrier bitch, who in 1853 killed 500 rats in $1\frac{1}{2}$ hours. Another mighty hunter was the so-called Red River Killer of Australia, a dingo cross weighing 112 lb and measuring 6 feet long, who killed more than 1000 sheep and 940 cattle over a period of ten years before being destroyed.

In the water the dog is generally a no more than adequate swimmer, employing the paddle stroke which is named after him and which is favoured by the majority of other species of landlubber mammal from pig to porcupine. There is one canine, however, who really is a most excellent swimmer and diver. This is the wild racoon dog (*Nyctereutes procyonoides*) of China, Japan and the Amur region of Siberia. An expert fisherman, the racoon dog can stay underwater for several minutes when in pursuit of his lunch.

VISION

This sense is quite well developed in dogs, although most species do not hunt primarily by sight and often 'miss' creatures which stand stock still. Against this it must be said that shepherds claim that their working dogs will react to purely visual hand signals at distances of one mile. Certainly dogs do not perceive the world about them as we do. Although not totally colour blind, they see mainly in black, white and various shades of grey. It can safely be said that the rhinestone-trimmed sunglasses sold for top dogs in New York and California are a dog-owner's status symbol rather than a summer aid for squinting, beach-bound Snoopies; and the only case I know of where an owner had contact lenses manufactured, for a hound whose cataractous eyes had been operated on, went wrong when the expensive slivers of optical glass slipped out onto the animal's nose, were licked into its mouth, ground up and swallowed!

TASTE

Dogs are gourmands rather than gourmets. They gobble rather than savour, swallow more than chew. Thus, as we would expect, Fido's sense of taste is relatively poorly developed.

SMELL

A leaflet was circulated among Vietcong guerillas fighting in Vietnam in 1962, giving advice on countering the war dogs employed by the US Army: 'To make the dogs lose their sense of direction when they are chasing us, confuse their sense of smell with mixed odours. Garlic, onions, perfumes like eau-de-cologne and overripe pepper-corns will all make difficulties for them. When we camouflage ourselves we should use these items by spreading them either on our

bodies or over the vent holes of our underground hideouts.
When in close combat, aromatic foods like fried fish and
roasted meats can be thrown to the dog to put him off. You
should also discard your sweating jacket or shirt to distract
him.'

The mind boggles at the thought of those battle-hardened
little men in black pyjamas slipping through the jungle
equipped to the teeth with ropes of onions, perfume sprays,
garlic and ammunition boxes bulging with fried fish. Does
this document reveal the secret of their eventual success?
Was it due to the fact that no adversary could stand up to an
assault by folk smelling like a mixture of Miss Dior,
bouillabaisse and a Lancashire chip shop?

Whatever the truth of the matter, the above excerpt contains both accurate and inaccurate assumptions regarding
the canine sense of smell.

Dogs are marvellous smellers. Although it varies from
breed to breed and among individuals in any one breed,
their olfactory ability is outstanding and far superior to that

of ourselves – in fact about one million times better. (Only eels are better smellers than dogs, while butterflies have a sense of smell approximately equal in sensitivity to dogs but can use it at much longer distances!) Dogs are used in France and Italy to find the subterranean truffle fungus, in Holland and Denmark to detect gas leaks. They are more accurate than the most sensitive odour-measuring machines and are used everywhere to search for humans, explosives and drugs, often under incredible conditions. An Alsatian of the Cairo police successfully followed the track of a donkey that had been made $4\frac{1}{2}$ days previously.

How do they do it?

Smells consist of molecules of particular chemicals floating in the air. When these molecules land on the special olfactory membrane inside a nose, nerve impulses convey the 'smell information' to a particular part of the brain. This olfactory centre is highly developed in the dog and relatively far larger than in man. The olfactory area in the adult human nose is about 3 square centimetres, whereas in the average canine nose it covers almost 130 square centimetres, being arranged in anatomical folds which filter smells from the incoming air. To accommodate such a structure, and with some recent exceptions among 'artificial' breeds, dogs have developed long noses. Even more important, there are vastly more sensory cells in the dog's olfactory membrane than there are in the human's. We have 5,000,000 sensory cells. A dachshund has 125,000,000, a fox terrier 147,000,000 and an alsatian 220,000,000.

A wet nose helps smelling; it dissolves molecules floating in the air, bringing them into contact with the olfactory membrane, and clears old smells away. For this reason another excellent smeller, the hedgehog, can often be seen to develop a runny nose when a stranger enters the room. Pigment helps smelling, too. How this works is not understood. The pigment is not in the sensory cells but lies nearby: dogs have dark nasal membranes and the black pigment in the nose pad may also play some part in increasing the dog's sense of smell.

Dogs can detect very faint smells, even when masked by a

more pungent odour. Truffle hounds (like wild boar, wild cats, wolves, bears, deer, goats, badgers and rabbits, which also relish the delicacy and actively seek it out) can find the fungus even though it may grow twelve inches underground. Only one human being has ever been known to be able to smell out truffles in this way. Oh to be a dog, with black truffles worth £90 a lb!

Every individual, be he human, deer or dormouse, has a sweat which is as unique to him as his fingerprints. It is made up of a number of different-smelling fatty acids. A dog can recognise the 'scent image' of a person and can even make important deductions from the evaporation of various ingredients of the smell with time. This allows him to run along a trail for a few yards, register the change in the image and thus determine the direction of travel of his quarry.

One of the common fatty acids present in sweat, butyric acid, is also found in the body of any dead animal and, if eaten, produces an enhanced sense of smell four to five days after the meal. At such times the sense of smell may be three times more acute than usual. This mechanism is invaluable to the wild dogs; they eat, taking in the butyric acid, and then in a few days, when they are hungry once more, the chemical has got their noses into tip-top form, ready for the next hunt.

HEARING

Something else at which dogs are excellent. Equipped with large external ears that are served by seventeen muscles, they can prick and swivel these sound receivers to focus on the source of any noise. They can register sounds of 35,000 vibrations per second (compared to 20,000 per second in man and 25,000 per second in the cat), are sensitive enough to be able to differentiate between, for example, two metronomes, one ticking at 100 beats per minute and the other at 96 beats per minute, and can shut off their inner ear so as to filter from the general din those sounds on which they want to concentrate. (This gift makes them ideal cocktail party-goers.)

OTHER EQUIPMENT

Though a dog's sense of balance is not to be compared with that of a cat, he uses his whiskers, when he has them, in a similar way. They act as delicate, touch-sensitive antennae that are particularly useful in the dark. Swing a longish-whiskered dog in your arms and you will find that the whiskers move forward as the animal does, feeling out the space in front of the moving animal.

Like cats, dogs are very sensitive to vibrations and will give warning of earth tremors some time, and occasionally even days, before humans are aware of any movement in the ground. In 1853 the British meteorologist, Admiral Robert Fitzroy, wrote: 'In the town of Concepción on the Pacific Coast of Chile at 11.30 am the dogs fled out of the houses. Ten minutes later an earthquake destroyed the town.' The curious thing is that dogs react like this only to the imminence of true earthquakes; somehow they can tell the difference between the advance tremors of the real thing and the 150,000 other vibrations of the earth's crust which occur

each year and which cause the animals to show not the slightest alarm. Instruments cannot tell the difference between the two kinds of tremor; how does Fido do it? No one yet knows.

The dog comes equipped with one efficient weapons system – its teeth. The powerful jaw muscles provide a hefty bite if required. A 44-lb mongrel has been found to exert a bite of 363 lb pressure. The average human adult can gnaw no harder than 45–65 lb, with some strong men reaching 160 lb, and the record is held by a Frenchman who achieved 534 denture-pulverising pounds. A 120-lb crocodile has been measured to clamp down when annoyed with 1540 lb and the tiger is thought to chomp away at around the 1700–1800 lb mark.

Finally, what about extra sensory perception in dogs? I don't want to enter the thorny thicket of debate as to whether or not dogs can see ghosts, but many psychic investigators claim evidence that a telepathic rapport has

been set up between a man and his dog. Try giving your dog mental commands when you are sitting down with your eyes closed. Call him to you, tell him to fetch a particular toy. Concentrate on it, but beware of giving your pet minute sensory clues through your body language. Dogs are keen observers at close range, so to carry out such experiments seriously, animal and man should be out of sight and sound of one another. Nevertheless, after repeated testing under apparently stringent conditions, certain canine telepaths do seem to exist.

3

The 'Historiam et observat. Medico-physicarum', a medical treatise published in 1676, reported a three-headed dog being born in Bavaria. All three of the heads possessed the ability to suckle but despite this the strange monster, a real-life Cerberus, died at the age of six days.

Acquiring a Dog

All the care and consideration that goes into picking that dumbest of family pets, the automobile, needs to be brought into play when planning to acquire a pooch. As when buying a car, you need to ask yourself certain questions. What do I want it to do? How much fuel will it burn? Garaging? Can I afford to have it serviced regularly? Can I drive (exercise) the model I have in mind?

Alsatians and borzois are not for a sixteenth-floor flatlet, great danes eat as much meat as a two-year old lion, Afghan hounds demand constant coiffing. Think first. Think hard.

If you haven't got the space or the inclination to jog with your dog or if there isn't an abundance of cash around, then think small – a toy or small breed.

If it's a companion, friend or watchdog you need, why go for a pedigree anyway? Mongrels are cheap, come in all sizes, give and take as much love and affection as any blue-blood and may well have that inbuilt aid to health that scientists call 'hybrid vigour'.

Some pedigrees may have the shape, proportions and colour that breeders intend and admire but are also heir to the unwelcome hereditary problems that go along with their aristocracy as surely as haemophilia ran through some of the Royal Houses of Europe. The long backs of dachshunds are just asking for slipped disc troubles; alsatians can have hereditary hip-joint disease; red setters get problems in the retinas of their eyes more frequently than do other breeds; the squashed face of the bulldog makes it prone to skin disease between the pugilist's folds of skin; the hairy ear canals of poodles are sitting ducks for canker infection, and so on and so on. All of these complaints, of course, can and do crop up in mongrels, but they're just not as likely.

Go to a breeder, answer an advertisement in the newspaper or magazine or contact the nearest dogs' home. Avoid pet shops or the sort of puppy farm that churns out animals like a sausage machine; they are so often reservoirs of serious disease. If it's a pedigree you're after, you'll have to trust the breeder or take along someone who has experience of that particular breed when making the purchase. Remember, it is not likely that you'll be provided with a Cruft's champion, no matter what you pay. It is difficult with young puppies for anyone, even an expert, to spot a future star. Why you need your reliable breeder or experienced companion is to make sure that you aren't palmed off with the runt of the litter ('Why not have this dinky littlest one, he's ever so sweet?') or one that shows faulty congenital features such as white spots on a breed that should be all-black, or an imperfect set of teeth. True, the poodle with one pale blue and one dark brown eye may have the cutest expression and he'll still be an attractive, robust pet, but you shouldn't be paying the price that a show-worthy individual would fetch.

The main thing, assuming that you are not rescuing a homeless animal, is to ensure that the dog is fit. Whatever you do, let the vet examine it as soon as possible afterwards. When selecting a pup look for:

Lively, fussy behaviour.
Clean nose, eyes and ears with no signs of discharge. A clear drop of 'water' from the nostrils is OK.
Pink gums, tongue and inside the eyelids.
No sign of diarrhoea – look at the stools if present.
Is the area around the anus and the hair of the hind-legs

fouled with loose droppings?
No spots, sores or scales in the coat or on the hair-free belly.
No cough.

If the vendor comes up with some tale of 'He's just getting over a bit of a cold, but it's nothing', or 'Don't worry about that tummy rash, you always get that in tripehounds', prick up your ears. No matter how eminent the breeder, have the 'cold' or the 'rash' checked out at once by the vet. Best of all, postpone the deal until the allegedly trivial ailment has cleared up.

If the pup (or an older animal) is sold as having been vaccinated, make sure you receive a certificate to that effect, signed by a registered veterinarian. If there is any doubt about whether the animal has been vaccinated, have it done again to be sure.

Of course, if you are taking in a stray or unwanted animal things are slightly different. You may have to deal with an already sick or infirm individual. But you are going into this worthwhile relationship with your eyes open, and the vet will advise you at the outset as to what problems you may have to face.

If your new pet is a puppy, see the Pup Servicing Schedule on pages 51–3.

Garaging your pet, certainly while it is a puppy, means indoors with the family. Later, if you want to re-house the dog in an outside kennel, buy or have built a good-quality residence with enough but not too much space: the minimum length is the length of your dog plus half its breadth; the minimum breadth is twice the breadth of the dog; and the minimum height is the standing height of the dog to the top of its head. The kennel must have well-insulated walls and roof and a floor that is raised from the ground by at least a few inches. It must be dry, draught-proof and easily

cleanable. The door should be just big enough for the full-grown animal and there must be disposable bedding – preferably old newspapers. Indoors, the dog needs a bed or basket in a convenient, draught-free spot, again supplied with layers of newspaper as bedding. An animal should have its own crockery, preferably made of stainless steel or solid earthenware.

The only other pieces of essential equipment are a lead, a collar and something for the dog to chew on – one of the cow-hide 'bones' sold in pet shops for example. Most important, straightaway, is to attach a disc on the collar. This should show, as well as his address, your pet's name.

A traditional and most polite greeting in China when entering someone's home was to ask, 'What is the honour-able name of your dog?' This applied even where, as in most cases, no dog was owned. The old habit of keeping house-dogs had declined and, instead, pottery figures of dogs were used to 'guard' the dwelling. Nevertheless, the genteel etiquette of enquiring after the substitute pet continued up until recent years.

Fashions in pet dogs' names don't change all that much. 'Brutus' (like Landseer's dog which can be seen in his picture, 'The Invader of the Larder'), 'Bo'sun' (Lord Byron's faithful companion) and 'Boy' (Prince Rupert's hound that was killed at the Battle of Marston Moor) are still favourite names.

The trade of dog 'finding' was carried out in mid-nineteenth century London by men picturesquely and accurately called 'lurkers'. One famous member of this shady profession was Chelsea George, whose success at the work was attributed to the special mixture of fried, minced liver and tincture of myrrh with which he varnished his hands before setting out, odorously, to 'lurk'. A contemporary writer described George's modus operandi thus: 'Chelsea George caresses every animal who seems a likely "spec", and when his fingers have been rubbed over the dogs' noses they become easy and perhaps willing captives. A bag carried for the purpose receives the victim, and away goes George, bag and all, to his printer's in Seven Dials. Two bills and no

less – two and no more, for such is George's *style* of work – are issued to describe the animal that has thus been found, and which will be restored to its owner on payment of expenses. One of these George puts in his pocket, the other he pastes up at a public-house whose landlord is "fly" to its meaning, and poor "bow-wow" is sold to a dealer in dogs not very far from Sharp's Alley. In course of time the dog is discovered, the possessor refers to the establishment where he bought it, the dealer makes himself "square" by giving the address of the chap he bought it off, and Chelsea George shows a copy of the advertisement, calls in the publican as a witness and leaves the place without the slightest imputation on his character.'

By this stratagem this king among 'lurkers' earned on average £150 per annum – quite a tidy fortune.

4

Even without table scraps and other leftovers which cannot have a value put on them, the dog-owners of Great Britain spend £430,000,000 on food for their animals each year.

Fuel for your Dog

The Canid family certainly love their pound, or in the case of tinier species like the fennec their ounce, of flesh. But it would be a mistake to regard our dog friends as narrow-minded carnivores. The coyote has a tooth for fruit and adores water-melon, even when it is unripe. Foxes have a catholic taste that ranges through grubs, rodents, snakes, crayfish, mushrooms, acorns and various sorts of fruit. The jackal augments his diet with vegetables, fruit and sugar cane. The bat-eared fox goes dotty for termites and the Chilean wild dog is a shellfish addict, catching, cracking and consuming large numbers of crab. It is true to say, in short, that the family is fairly omnivorous and indeed they are equipped for this life-style with quite large 'tubercular', crunching teeth at the back of their mouths which can deal with vegetable matter when flesh is scarce.

The domestic dog, like his wild cousins, needs more than meat in his dish to keep him going. His requirements and fancies can be catered for easily enough if you follow certain simple rules and throw away the innumerable tomes that have been written by fanatical breeders of one sort or another, pluggers of esoteric vegetarian or herbal regimes and the bright young men of pet-food advertising agencies. The basic rules, as I say, are simple and there are many alternative ways of building up a correct food programme that pleases both Bonzo and his faithful owner. It is not a theological matter, as some folk imply, but plain common sense. Victualling a Cruft's winner is based on the same

principles as those for a Pennine farmer's sheepdog or a pensioner's mongrel pup. There is no special diet for a borzoi and another for a pekingese. 'Food for pedigree dogs' and 'Formulated for show champions' are the weasel words of the PR man – rubbish.

THE DOG NEEDS CERTAIN THINGS

These are:

Protein. For body building and repair. Found in meat, fish, eggs, cheese, beans, nuts.

Carbohydrates. For energy. Found in starchy foods, cereals, bread, potatoes, honey.

Fats. For energy and good health of skin and hair. Found in meat, fish, nuts, certain seeds, milk, cheese.

Vitamins. For certain essential chemical reactions in the body. Found in a balanced diet and some, vitamin C and possibly vitamin K, are manufactured within the body itself.

Bulk. For good digestive and bowel action. Found in vegetables, some forms of cereal.

Water. For all processes occurring everywhere in the body.

Before dealing with practicalities, we must consider briefly a few crucial bits of theory.

Apart from age, degree of activity, environment (centrally heated flatlet or farmyard kennel), pregnancy, lactation and disease, any of which markedly alters an animal's requirements, we must never forget that dogs, like their owners, are all individuals. Just as in people, some of whom get fat though eating moderately while others stay slim on twice the amount of cream cakes and ale, each dog varies in his degree of efficiency in burning or storing foodstuffs. But as a rule of thumb we can say that a dog needs the following daily amounts of calories at different periods in his life:

Puppy	100 calories per lb body weight
Adult	50–70 calories per lb body weight
OAP	25 calories per lb body weight

These figures are calculated for moderately active animals.

The calories come mainly from the carbohydrates and fat in the food. The proportions of protein, carbohydrate and fat in the complete diet need careful attention. Too high a proportion of fat will upset the bowels, too low may affect skin condition. Too high a proportion of fat and carbohydrate at the expense of protein results in the obesity found in so many modern dogs, while too little of these prime energy-givers forces the dog to burn expensive protein as a makeshift energy source. Apart from hitting your pocket this will deprive your pet of essential minerals and bulk.

So we must arrange the proportions by weight so that the diet consists roughly of:

Protein 20 per cent (of which at least half must be of animal origin)
Carbohydrate 70–75 per cent
Fat 5–10 per cent

THE SORTS OF THINGS DOGS CAN EAT

We all know the dog down at the pub who is partial to his nightly half of old ale, and the poodle with a penchant for strawberries. In general, I am all for keeping a dog's dinner as varied as possible. Certain allergies and idiosyncracies apart, there is little that his master eats that Fido should not or, indeed, will not delight in sharing. There are so many myths, fables and conflicting opinions about feeding a dog: eggs either are or are not taboo; potatoes either can or cannot be digested; bones either are or are not good for

the teeth; meat must be fed either raw or cooked. The truth is that, remaining moderate of course in all things, there are remarkably few firm do's and don'ts in feeding your pet.

Before looking at the main types of diet, here are some of the ingredients that can be used.

Meat. Meat of all kinds, including offal, is one of the most important canine foodstuffs. Raw or cooked? Ideally your pet should become accustomed to having both – raw sometimes, cooked at others. Naturally, raw meat carries a risk of bacterial infection but this is not great if you buy it fresh from a butcher. Do not use raw knacker's meat. Offal such as tripe is best cooked and then chopped up.

Meat is low in calcium and rich in phosphorus. Lean meat is too low in fat to be fed in large quantities: an all-lean-meat diet would be nutritionally very unbalanced as well as expensive. Liver contains abundant quantities of protein, iron and vitamins but can be too much for the digestive tract. It should not exceed 5 per cent of the total diet.

Fish. Packed with protein, minerals and, in some cases, fats. Best fed cooked. Raw herring and mackerel can deprive the dog's body of vitamin B_1. It is best to remove the large bones from most kinds of fish, but they can safely be left in herring, mackerel and the smaller fish.

Cheese and milk products. Rich in protein, fat and minerals. Some dogs cannot digest lactose (milk sugar) due to the absence of an enzyme in their bodies. Such intolerance of milk, producing diarrhoea and occasionally vomiting, is not serious: simply take milk off your pet's diet.

Cereals. Either as meals (bran, oats, maize etc) or in biscuit form, these are an inexpensive source of energy, bulk, minerals and some vitamins. Cooked rice is an excellent substitute.

Vegetables. Yes, dogs can handle starch in potatoes very well. It is as good a foodstuff for them as for man but as for man, it will obviously lead to problems if over-indulged in. Other vegetables such as carrots, cabbage, turnip, swede are valuable, either cooked or shredded raw.

Fruit. Dogs make their own vitamin C internally, but they do benefit from moderate quantities of any fruit from time to time.

Eggs. Whole egg should be fed cooked to avoid the effect of an anti-vitamin B factor present in raw white egg. Egg yolk can be fed raw.

Other things. Nuts, edible seeds, honey are all excellent additions to the diet. And if your pet insists on chewing and swallowing grass and herbs let him, even if it seems to make him vomit shortly afterwards. It is perfectly natural.

Question-mark foods

Bones are a knotty problem. No, they don't clean the teeth. The reason why wild dog or sheepdog teeth are so clean isn't due to bone-crunching but to the cleaning effect of biting through hair and skin – plus the fact that they don't get sweetmeats very often.

Bones are not essential to the canine diet if it is properly balanced. They can cause problems such as constipation, obstruction or perforation. The best advice, therefore, is to restrict any bones given to the broad, marrow-bone type, although in my experience less trouble comes from the splintery bones (like those from poultry) than from the more substantial bones like sheep's neck, vertebrae or pigs' knuckles which may be bolted whole.

Sweets, chocolates, puddings, cakes. These have all the advantages and disadvantages that they have for human children except that they are not in any way implicated in canine caries (tooth decay) – a very rare condition. However, soft food does promote the build-up of tartar, or plaque, round the dog's teeth. This is common and often leads to mouth problems. But as the occasional treat? Why not!

Bread, like potatoes, is no worse or better for dogs than it is for humans. It can be fed as part of a balanced diet. There is no need to worry about giving white bread in dogs: it will not cause fits or other brain damage. The chemical called agene which was the cause of some trouble in dogs many years ago is no longer used in the baking of white bread. As with humans, wholemeal bread will provide more bulk for the healthy exercise of the dog's intestine.

Supplements

Do you need vitamins, minerals, condition powders, etc, for your pet? The answer is emphatically no, as long as you are providing a good, balanced diet. Exceptions are pregnant and lactating bitches, pups and some geriatric cases (see page 60). For these groups a multivitamin or mineral capsule, powder or drops will be recommended by your veterinary surgeon. You can do positive harm by loading a dog up with far more vitamins than he needs. Overdosing vitamin D, a chemical involved in the production of bone, may cause your pet to deposit bone in strange places like the heart for kidneys, and too much vitamin A can actually poison. 'Condition powders', 'blood salts', sulphur blocks in the water bowl and so on are unnecessary catchpennies.

THE DIET ITSELF: ALTERNATIVE SYSTEMS

Do-it-yourself

The 'do-it-yourself' – meat, scraps and biscuit – system is still popular, gives variety and may be economic. Its obvious disadvantage is the risk of a lack of balanced nutrients in the hotch-potch. If you persist in following this method, try at least to remember some of the basic principles listed above and see that the daily intake of meat is about ½ oz per lb body weight per day for young animals and ⅓ oz per lb for adults. Bear in mind also that cooked table scraps, including vegetables, may lack vitamins, which are destroyed by heat. Include some uncooked ingredients.

Commercial foods

Canned food. Forty per cent of all food bought for dogs in Great Britain is in tins, at an average weekly expenditure of around 63p per pet. Canned food is of two types, the wholly meaty kind that contains very little carbohydrate, and the complete diet which consists of meat, carbohydrates, fat, minerals and vitamins in correct balance. The first kind is not to be fed as the only food for your pet. It is essentially conveniently packed, sterile, vitaminised meat. It contains a variable amount of water depending on the brand and is not

particularly cheap. Dog biscuits or meal must be added to make a complete diet at a rate of one part of tinned meat to one part of biscuit for small breeds or one part of tinned meat to two parts of biscuit for bigger breeds. Approximate quantities of tinned meat per day: toy breeds $\frac{1}{2}$–$\frac{3}{4}$ can, small breeds $\frac{3}{4}$–$1\frac{1}{2}$ cans, medium breeds $1\frac{1}{2}$–$2\frac{1}{2}$ cans, large breeds $2\frac{1}{2}$–4 cans. I refer here to large size cans containing $13\frac{1}{2}$–$14\frac{1}{2}$ oz.

The complete diet tinned foods have mainly been produced as the result of careful nutritional research by the big pet-food companies. They don't need anything added to them and should be fed at the rates recommended on the can label. This is usually around 10 oz for a 5-lb dog, 2 lb for a 25-lb specimen and $4\frac{1}{4}$ lb for a 70-lb heavyweight. This system is ideal for the owner in a hurry but is certainly the most expensive.

Although, surprisingly, some dogs will continue to scoff nothing but cans of 'Wizzo' or 'Soopa Doopa' year in, year out without tiring of the monotonous taste, other canines are more gastronomically inclined and demand change. A few ultra-fussy individuals treat their owners like a dowager duchess arranging the week's menu with the head cook. Such animals, commoner among the fancy breeds, need frequent variations: small quantities of freshly opened small tins at several times throughout the day. Whatever diet you use, never let food become stale.

Remember, too, that whatever the theoretical requirements or appetite of your dog may be, it is essential to keep an eye on his or her waistline.

Completely balanced dry foods. These pellets, 'nuts' or biscuits of dried food contain meat and/or fish products together with carbohydrates, minerals and vitamins. They are economical, easy to store and convenient. Unfortunately, many dogs do not like the taste or quickly tire of them. They are *not* to be confused with simple dog biscuits or meals which are largely cereal in content and do not provide a complete diet. As ever, a plentiful supply of fresh water is essential. Amounts to feed:

Weight of dog	Daily weight of complete dry food
5 lb	approx 4 oz
25 lb	9 oz
70 lb	1 lb 3 oz

Semi-moist complete food. This modern, highly processed, often 'plastic'-looking food is perfectly balanced and possibly the most convenient of doggy convenience foods. It is relatively non-messy. As value for money it falls between the dry and canned foods but does not store as long as either. Sachets of soft-moist food containing approximately 6 oz of food should be fed as follows:

Weight of dog	Daily number of sachets
5 lb	$\frac{1}{2}-\frac{3}{4}$
25 lb	$1\frac{1}{2}-2\frac{1}{2}$
70 lb	$2\frac{1}{2}-4$

WHICH DIET TO CHOOSE?

All diets have their advantages. There is no reason why you should not switch from one to the other according to Fido's fads and fancies. If you find that one scheme is well received by your pet and has no drawbacks, by all means stick to it. Remember always to prepare food freshly and serve it in thoroughly cleaned dishes. Clean, fresh water should be permanently available.

HOW MANY MEALS A DAY?

One or two. There is no absolute rule. I prefer to split the daily requirement into two parts and feed twice. Nutrition isn't everything; why shouldn't your dog start the day with a full tummy and go to bed likewise?

In Victorian days, London dog-owners were served by purveyors of pet meat who called themselves 'carriers'. Dressed in shiny hats, black plush waistcoats, blue aprons and corduroy trousers, and sporting one to three blue-and-white spotted handkerchiefs around their necks, these gentlemen would walk up to forty miles each day doing their rounds. The meat was sold on small skewers at a farthing, halfpenny and a penny each, or in bigger pieces at $2\frac{1}{2}$d per lb.

In 1845 one carrier declared, 'Mine's a middling trade, but some does far better. Some cats has a ha'porth a day, some every other day; very few can afford a penn'orth, but times is inferior. Dogs is better pay when you've a connection among 'em. The best districts are among the houses of tradesmen, mechanics and labourers. The coachmen in the mews at the back of the squares are very good customers. Old maids are bad, though very plentiful, customers. They cheapen the carriers down so, that they can scarcely live at the business. They will pay one halfpenny and owe another, and forget that after a day or two.'

5

The Assembly-line: the Patter of Little Paws

Domestic dogs are generally very promiscuous although there is evidence that the beagle does show a certain degree of mate preference. Wolves, jackals and coyotes, on the other hand, are highly respectable, show strong mate preference and fidelity and very rarely indulge in promiscuity under normal, free-living conditions.

The bitch usually becomes sexually mature somewhere between 8 and 12 months of age. It may be as early as 6 months in some cases, or be delayed until 18 months. If a bitch has not had her first 'heat' period by 20 months of age it is wise to consult your veterinarian.

The bitch comes into 'heat' (sometimes called 'season') when her sexual cycle, controlled by her glands, reaches a certain phase. The heat is generally 18–21 days long although the bitch will only accept the dog and conceive during a few days around the middle of the heat period. The first stage of heat is indicated by puffiness of the lips of the vulva. Soon bleeding begins (this is in no way the equivalent of the menstrual period in human females). During this time, which may last 4–14 days with an average of 10 days, the bitch is highly attractive to dogs but will not accept their advances.

Following this stage, the bleeding diminishes or ceases altogether, the vulva attains maximum enlargement and the

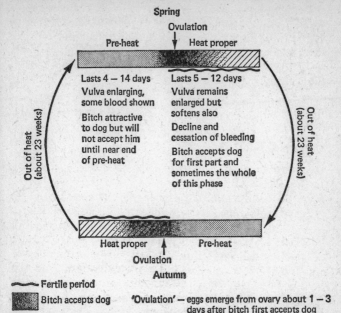

Spring

Ovulation

Pre-heat ← | → Heat proper

Lasts 4 — 14 days

Vulva enlarging, some blood shown

Bitch attractive to dog but will not accept him until near end of pre-heat

Lasts 5 — 12 days

Vulva remains enlarged but softens also

Decline and cessation of bleeding

Bitch accepts dog for first part and sometimes the whole of this phase

Out of heat (about 23 weeks)

Out of heat (about 23 weeks)

Heat proper | ← | Pre-heat

Ovulation

Autumn

~~~~ Fertile period

▓▓ Bitch accepts dog

'Ovulation' — eggs emerge from ovary about 1 — 3 days after bitch first accepts dog

bitch will accept the dog. This is the fertile period and lasts 5–12 days with sexual desire at its most marked during the first 2–3 days. When the bleeding fades away and the bitch first allows the dog to press his suit, that is the time to allow mating to take place if you are planning to have puppies. Mating should be repeated two days later to increase the chance of a successful fertilisation. If a bitch conceives during mating, the heat period tends to end more quickly than otherwise.

Heat normally occurs twice a year except in Basenjis which, like the wild dogs, foxes and wolves, have only one sexual cycle per year. Although you can find bitches which come into heat at other times, there is a tendency for a spring heat to occur in January–March, with the autumn heat during August–September. These are averages, remember. Exceptions frequently occur. Some bitches may have somewhat longer or shorter intervals between successive heats.

Hormones such as megestrol, given by mouth or injection, can be used to halt a heat, to postpone it or to suppress the sexual cycle altogether. There are special precautions that must be observed when considering these hormone applications and you must be guided by your vet in choosing the best course for your animal.

COMMONLY ASKED QUESTIONS

Q. *When my bitch is in 'heat', how can I stop neighbouring dogs pestering her?*

A. Never let her run out on her own. Exercise her on the lead. Spray the bitch's rear parts with a special deodorant aerosol obtainable from the pet shop, or dab on a little oil of citronella. Do the same to your doorstep and garden gate. Repeat at least daily.

Q. *If my bitch is accidentally mated by a dog, how do I avoid an unwanted pregnancy?*

A. An injection of an oestrogen hormone by the vet within four days of the mating will sort that out. Try not to make a habit of it, however, as too many such shots may have long-term ill effects on the bitch's womb.

Q. *If my pedigree bitch is accidentally mated by an ill-bred loutish mongrel, is she spoiled for future breeding?*

A. Certainly not.

Q. *If my bitch, which for years has had regular intervals between heats, suddenly becomes erratic with much shorter or longer intervals or prolonged bleeding, is there anything to worry about?*

A. It may be the sign of imminent ovary or womb trouble. Consult your vet.

Q. *Should I breed from my bitch's first heat period?*

A. No. Wait until the second one at least.

Q. *Should every bitch have at least one litter of pups in her life?*

A. It all depends on your circumstances. If you are really sure that you will never want puppies around the house, it is best to have the bitch sterilised (spayed). A serious womb disease called pyometra is very common in bitches that have never had a litter of pups. It occurs less frequently in bitches that have had one litter and infrequently in ones that have had more than one. Spaying avoids all such possibilities. See pages 55–6.

Q. *Does venereal disease occur in dogs?*

A. Yes, but not the kind that can afflict humans or other animals. There is a transmissable venereal tumour of dogs, now less common than in the past.

Q. *Can artificial insemination be used in dogs?*

A. Yes. It is a relatively simple technique that is sometimes used when breeding difficulties arise.

Q. *Do bitches have a sort of menopause like women?*

A. Not really. Heats may become less frequent and milder in very old bitches and fertility may drop, with only small litters of pups produced, but there is no equivalent to the human menopause.

Q. *What is the largest litter of pups recorded?*

A. Twenty-three, with a possible but unauthenticated twenty-four.

Q. *Why do dogs get 'stuck together' when mating?*

A. There is a special 'bulb' in the canine penis which swells up and 'locks' it inside the vagina of the bitch during mating. Withdrawal is not possible until the congested bulb has shrunk back to normal. Throwing buckets of cold water over 'tied' dogs is cruel and can result in wrenching damage to the animals' organs as they try to pull apart. Let the creatures part in their own good time.

Q. *Some dogs are 'shy breeders'; can anything be done to help? Are there canine aphrodisiacs?*

A. Young, inexperienced animals often need time, encouragement and sometimes actual help from their owners before managing to get their mating right. Some otherwise normal dogs with a low sex drive may be helped by tablets of yohimbine extract prescribed by the veterinarian.

PREGNANCY

The length of pregnancy is on average sixty-three days. During this time the bitch will lay down extra fat stores under the skin and within her belly in preparation for nursing the babies. Any rise in weight due to this fat is usually lost progressively throughout the nursing period. The pups themselves do not contribute much to the mother's increase in weight until after the fifth week of pregnancy. Swelling of the tummy becomes increasingly more noticeable from the fifth week onwards, although where only one or two pups are being carried, or the bitch is plump anyway, this sign of approaching maternity may be difficult to spot.

The vet can diagnose pregnancy by carefully feeling the bitch's abdomen. There are at present no blood or urine tests for pregnancy in the bitch.

The breasts enlarge and the teats become larger and pinker from about the thirty-fifth day of pregnancy. A watery secretion can be drawn from the teats 3-4 days

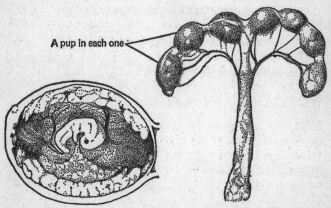

A pup in each one

Foetus (exposed) from the uterus at 25 days   Canine uterus at 25 days before the pups are born. In bitches which have had several litters, enlargement of the breasts may not begin until the last week of pregnancy and true milk can often be produced as early as 5–6 days before the onset of labour.

What you must do during your bitch's pregnancy
1 Feed her extra quantities of protein, energy and mineral-containing foods – meat, fish, eggs and cereals.
2 Continue giving her plenty of exercise right up to the end.
3 Add multivitamins and calcium salts to the diet as prescribed by your veterinarian.
4 Get things ready for the arrival of the puppies. The whelping and nursing mum will need quiet, clean accommodation in a box, basket or kennel, with lots of old newspapers on hand for disposable bedding. If you're new at the game, have a chat with a reliable breeder or your vet.
5 Don't give any drugs or medicines unless prescribed by the vet, except for a safe and reliable worming drug which is important to prevent infestation of the puppies with worms even while they are still within their mother's womb. The bitch should be given a course of mebendazole or piperazine tablets three times: at the very beginning of pregnancy, ten days before whelping and ten days after whelping.

WHELPING

If you are certain of the date of the last possible mating, don't worry if your bitch goes over the prescribed sixty-three days by a few days, provided she is eating and is generally well, has no coloured discharge (red, green, brown, cream or anything other than clear) from the vulva and has not been seen on any occasion to strain other than when passing a motion. But if any of these rules are broken and pups have not appeared within two hours, consult your vet.

When birth is imminent, the bitch becomes restless, pants fitfully and prepares her bed. This means that she wanders about, sometimes chooses a site quite different to the one you had in mind, paws fretfully at the bedding and turns round and round in pre-occupied circles before lying down, only to be up again in a short while. This stage of pre-labour usually lasts around twelve hours but it can be much briefer or go on, sometimes with intervals of a return to normal behaviour, for a day or two. If there is no straining, no coloured discharge, no matter how slight, from the vulva and the bitch is otherwise well in herself, all is in order.

Labour proper can be regarded as beginning when you see the first strain by the bitch or the appearance of a coloured (often bottle-green) discharge. Count from now. Within one hour the first pup should be born. A water-bag, which is generally ruptured by the licking of the bitch, comes first, followed by the puppy wrapped partly or entirely in its membranes. Puppies are often born back feet first; this is not a breech birth and is nothing to get alarmed about.

Once delivered, the puppy remains attached to the after-birth (placenta) until the mother bites it apart. If this doesn't occur, and particularly if the puppy's face is covered by the membrane, you can be of help. Clear the membrane away from the nostrils and face and break the umbilical cord. Don't use scissors. Pull the cord apart between the fingers of your two hands. Make the break about 1½ inches from the puppy's navel. *Don't* pull the cord away from the navel.

The bitch may rest between the birth of each successive pup for minutes or for hours. The intervals tend to get shorter as labour progresses, but may often be irregular.

The maximum time limit for the birth of any one pup, counting from the first strain or discharge which marks the beginning of labour proper, is two hours. Remember that this is two hours from the beginning of labour for that pup, not from the beginning of whelping. After the two hours is up, with the pup still undelivered, contact the vet.

The total time for whelping an average litter of four to eight pups is up to six hours. Even very big litters should not need more than twelve hours.

The afterbirths will be expelled either after each pup or

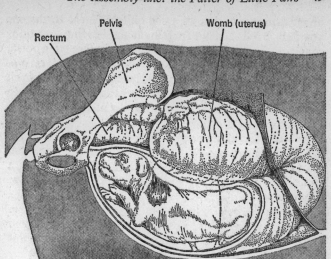

Rectum   Pelvis   Womb (uterus)

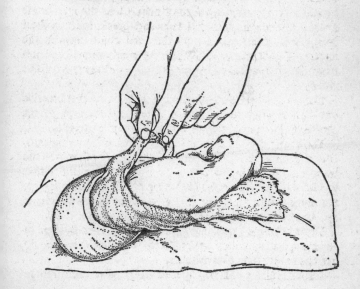

irregularly, coming in clumps at intervals or at the end of whelping. Try to avoid letting the bitch eat them, a natural instinct; burn or otherwise dispose of them.

Most bitches have no trouble in giving birth; where problems do arise the vet may help the animal manually, use drugs to dilate the birth canal or to strengthen contractions of the womb, or advise a Caesarian operation. This surgical procedure is done under general anaesthetic and is certainly to be recommended in most cases where labour has lasted longer than twelve hours. In these circumstances live puppies cannot be relied upon. Caesarian operation does not rule out future breeding and normal labour in subsequent whelpings.

Incidentally, the first recorded Caesarian operation on a living woman occurred in about AD 1500 and was performed by a Swiss pig-gelder on his wife. As early as 1824, successful Caesarians on the bitch were being carried out by Mr Hayes, a veterinary surgeon of Rochdale in Lancashire. This was at a time when the *Lancet* reported that only three out of the forty such operations on human patients in Great Britain up to that date had ended successfully.

You should only assist the bitch in labour where a puppy is half in and half out of the vulva and progressing slowly. Grasp the baby firmly with scrubbed hands and pull with a slight screwing action of the wrist. Pull smoothly and gently: don't jerk the pup. Try to pull along with any natural strainings of the bitch.

Remember that the black-green discharge associated with whelping is a normal feature of birth in the bitch. It doesn't occur in other species such as the cat.

CARE OF NEWBORN PUPPIES

The mother will do the lion's share of the work. You must provide her with a comfortable nursing box, daily changes of bedding such as layers of old newspaper or a blanket and washable cot sheet, and extra high-quality food.

If the bitch does not feed her pups for some reason or appears to have a shortage of milk, consult the vet. Often a simple injection of pituitary hormone can produce an immediate flow of milk where a mother has not been 'letting down' the nourishing liquid. Where necessary, puppies are easily reared on special canine milk powders such as Lactol or like human babies on Carnation milk, although the latter should be reconstituted with twice as much water as for babies.

PUP SERVICING SCHEDULE

Five to seven days old
The 'dew claws', the non-functioning toes found on the inside of the 'wrist' and 'ankle', which can cause trouble later through overgrowth of the claw or being injured while running, are best removed at this point. It is a simple matter and is performed by a veterinary surgeon or experienced breeder under aseptic conditions. Some breeds (Afghan hounds for example) do not have their dew claws removed. Tail docking, that mutilation which is done purely for the benefit of human vanity and the need to carve a dog into the shape demanded by arbitrary breed regulations,

should be done if you cannot avoid it at the same time. It is never necessary to dock cross-breds.

Three weeks old

Begin to introduce your puppies to small quantities of solid food such as puppy meal or cereals (Farex etc). These can be softened by adding warm milk or Lactol. Never rush changes in a puppy's diet as sudden alterations will produce stomach and bowel upsets. If such troubles should occur, give a teaspoonful of baby gripe water three times a day; if the upset isn't settled within twenty-four hours, see your vet.

Six weeks old

Weaning time. Puppies should now be weaned onto solid foods and this process should certainly be fully complete no later than ten weeks. Six weeks is the earliest at which a pup should be taken from its mother. At this point four meals a day should be provided and the quantities at each meal should be that which the little creature can scoff in about ten minutes. Always have plenty of clean drinking water available.

Specimen Menu (6–12 weeks of age):

Breakfast. Bowl of puppy meal, Farex or breakfast cereal with milk.

Lunch. Cooked mince meat, chopped tinned dog food, semi-moist food or proprietary balanced dried food.

Teatime. Milk. As for lunch, plus one drop of Abidec vitamin drops (from the chemist).

Evening meal. As for lunch, plus puppy meal, Farex or breakfast cereal with milk.

Eight weeks old

Worm the puppies using mebendazole, piperazine or

dichlorvos as prescribed by your vet. Don't try patent worm cures or Grandma's remedies. Modern worming drugs are safe, highly effective and non-messy.

Twelve weeks old

Vaccination time. It can be done earlier if the vet advises that there is some special risk of infection, but it will have to be repeated anyway at this stage of your puppy's life. *Until fourteen days after a puppy's first vaccination injection, keep it away from all dogs other than those in your own house and off the streets and parks.*

The puppy must be inoculated against Distemper (including Hardpad, a variety of Distemper), Contagious Canine Hepatitis, and the two forms of Leptospirosis (one which attacks the liver and the other the kidneys).

Keep your vaccination certificate in a safe place. Remember to have the dog boosted annually to keep his immunity high.

At present you are not allowed to have your dog vaccinated against Rabies in Great Britain, except under licence from the Ministry of Agriculture just before you take or send the animal abroad.

Three to six months old

Now give three meals a day.

Six months old

Buy the pup his first Dog Licence. Settle down to twice-a-day feeding.

HOUSE-TRAINING

From the moment you first interest the young puppy in solid food of any type, begin training him. It is stupid and wrong to rub a puppy's nose in his droppings or urine – that won't teach him a thing. Be patient: like a human infant, a puppy needs time to develop regular house-trained habits. Put him in a suitable spot immediately after each feed. Clear up at once any mess that he accidentally makes,

and spray the spot with a deodorant aerosol. This prevents him from being attracted back to the same place and 'triggered off' by lingering aromas to do the deed once more. Never punish a puppy for slowness in learning or for lapses in his mastery of lavatory etiquette.

FALSE PREGNANCY

It is quite common for a bitch with an unsullied reputation and certain virginity to exhibit signs of pregnancy where none exists. At around eight or nine weeks after being on heat, she will begin to show the restlessness, bed-making and fullness of the breasts that occur in truly pregnant mums. Milk may run from the teats and an old slipper, child's toy or lump of coal may be carefully tended, guarded and 'nursed' in the quiet place she has selected as her nursery. The animal is not consciously or unconsciously wanting to have puppies when this happens. It is not an illness. It will not result in ovary or womb disease. It may or may not occur following each six-monthly heat period.

The cause is the ovary which, having shed eggs during the heat period, carelessly assumes that fertilisation must have ensued as night follows day. It therefore goes about producing hormones that prepare the body for the arrival of the phantom puppies. Treatment is easy. Either let the phenomenon run its natural course (it will usually fade away after a couple of weeks or so) or see your vet. He may well prescribe a course of canine contraceptive pills which have the additional function of suppressing false pregnancies.

SPAYING

Neutering, sterilising, spaying: these are all words used for the ovariectomy operation which puts paid to bitches having unwanted pups. This procedure is irreversible, unlike the prevention of heat periods and pregnancy by contraceptive injections or pills. It is performed under general anaesthetic by a veterinary surgeon who will make a surgical incision either along the mid-line of the bitch's tummy or on one flank. It can be done at any age from twelve weeks onwards but is best left until after the animal's first heat period. It can be done during a heat period but this is not advisable unless there are special reasons; surgical operations during heat periods can be troublesome as there is a tendency for the bitch to bleed more easily when high levels of oestrogen sex hormones are circulating in her body.

Spayed bitches are not more prone to false pregnancies but less so. Their chances of breast cancer are reduced. Some do get fatter after the operation, but in my opinion this is more due to their owners over-indulging and under-exercising them than a direct effect of withdrawal of ovary hormones.

Spaying is *not* a cruel thing to do to a bitch; having unwanted pups and the pestering of in-heat bitches by hordes of ardent lovers can be. Spaying is no more 'unnatural' than having the dog vaccinated, clipped or bathed and has the major benefit that pyometra, the common and serious womb disease of middle and late age, is less likely after spaying.

Although not a cheap operation, spaying is an important once-and-for-all contribution to the well-being and longevity of your pet – if you're sure you never will want to breed from her. If in doubt, use the contraceptive pill for a year or two. Spaying can be done later when you make your mind up or when the bitch has had a litter or two of pups.

Veterans

One year of a dog's life is equivalent to seven of a man's: so the saying goes. It isn't true. A one-year-old bitch is mature and can have pups: a seven-year-old child cannot. Many dogs reach 15 years of age; few folk celebrate their 105th birthday. A more realistic approach has been worked out by a French veterinarian, Dr Lebeau. He suggests that the first year of a dog's life equals 15 human years, the second equals a further 9 human years and thereafter each dog year counts for 4 human years. This provides us with a table:

Age of dog	Equivalent age of man
1 yr	15 yrs
2 yrs	24 yrs
3 yrs	28 yrs
4 yrs	32 yrs
8 yrs	48 yrs
12 yrs	64 yrs
15 yrs	76 yrs
20 yrs	96 yrs

Like their owners, dogs are living longer nowadays, but few pass 17 years = 84 human years. The record for canine longevity is claimed for a 27¼-year-old black Labrador that died in 1963 in Boston, Lincolnshire, though there are less reliable reports of another dog tottering up to an incredible 34!

Special consideration needs to be given to the care of senior doggy citizens when they enter their teens.

OWNER AS WEIGHT-WATCHER

The dog days are those hot, humid days which in northern latitudes fall between 3 July and 11 August. The Greeks, Romans and Egyptians believed that Sirius, the Dog star, which rises simultaneously with the sun at this time, adds its heat to that of the sun to cause the high temperature. They also thought that dogs were subject to madness during these times. If by 'madness' they were referring to symptoms of heat-stroke that is often seen in hot weather, particularly in overweight dogs, they had a point.

Overweight animals won't live as long as they might. Obesity leads to heart trouble, liver inefficiency and diabetes. Your dog should keep a figure whose outline dips in behind the ribs to give the animal a distinctly separate chest and abdominal areas. Rolls of fat in the kidney area are to be discouraged. Apart from its direct ill-effects, excess fat makes more weight for old, arthriticky joints to bear. Cut out starch and carbohydrate foods when your pet begins to spread. Concentrate on meat, fish, eggs and vegetables. Shun on his behalf simple dog biscuits and meals, bread, potatoes, cereals and all sugary 'treats'. If he is a big milk drinker, withdraw it and make the dog stick to water – as much as he wants.

With really plump individuals I'm all for a serious crash course of dieting in their best interests. Every member of the family must be relied upon to co-operate; there must be no weakening of resolve, no giving in by Grandma to those soulful eyes that crave the traditional late-night chocolate drop. To register your (and your pet's) progress, weigh the dog once weekly. The simplest way is to stand on the bath-

GET OFF!

room scales with the creature in your arms. Then weigh yourself alone and work out the difference. A regular loss of five or six ounces per week is perfectly satisfactory. If you are worried that you might overdo the slimming process, stop when the ribs are just visible through the coat, or if your pet is a pedigree, ask a breeder what is the correct adult weight for your breed.

It is wise when contemplating the slimming of a grossly overweight animal to consult the vet first. He will advise you on the best approach for your animal and can make sure that the obesity is not being caused by a glandular fault or some other ailment.

Don't try human-type slimming pills on your pet. They don't work and can be bad for him.

The one simple method of slimming that your vet may prescribe is the use of special balanced obesity diets that come in cans like ordinary pet food but are low in calories and high in bulk.

Some older dogs go the other way and lose a great deal of weight. This may or may not be accompanied by an increase in appetite. At the first sign of weight loss in such cases, have the animal examined by the vet. A common cause is failing kidneys which 'leak' body protein away into the urine. You will need medical advice in maintaining a dog like this, but provided the dog has a good appetite, it will be OK in most cases to supply food containing readily available calories (human invalid foods such as 'Complan', bread, cereals, biscuit and potatoes) together with *small* quantities of high-quality protein (lean meat and fish) and vegetables. The vet may use one of the modern tissue-building (anabolic) hormones in these cases.

All older animals, and certainly those on either a slimming or weight-increasing regime, should receive an extra multivitamin supplement daily.

KIDNEYS

These important organs are among the first to show the effects of old age in the dog. If leptospirosis vaccination was properly carried out when the animal was young and has been boosted regularly throughout his life, the chances of chronic infectious nephritis, once a common killer, are remote. Keep the annual leptospirosis vaccine boosters up!

If the vet diagnoses kidney failure, do not despair. Apart from drugs, an intelligent diet for your pet can do much to let the animal live a normal, longer life. Cut the amount of protein in the rations to about 6 per cent. Use good-quality lean meat, egg and fish to supply this. The rest of the diet should be made up of such things as potatoes, rice, bread, cooked cereals, vegetables and fruit. Bouillon cubes should be used to make 'meaty' dishes out of the starchy foods and to provide salts to replace those which leak through the kidneys. Special tinned diets for kidney patients can be prescribed by your vet and are balanced with a $5\frac{1}{2}$ per cent protein content. There is absolutely no reason to restrict the dog's water intake. If he is more thirsty than before, let him drink. If he drinks so much at once that he tends to overload his stomach and vomit, give him a little water and often. Dogs in this condition must be regularly checked over by the vet.

'RHEUMATICKS'

When the suspension gets noisy and the wheels wobble, the dog needs as much attention as does the veteran car.

True rheumatism is uncommon in animals but arthritis frequently occurs in various forms. As with humans there is no absolute cure, but much can be done to relieve pain, keep the joints moving and reduce lameness. At the first sign of 'bad running', let the vet examine your animal. The whole range of anti-arthritic medicine from gold injections to corticosteroids to acupuncture to modern antiflammatory chemicals are being used to tackle the problem in dogs. For a quick emergency treatment of a painful, creaky joint give your dog $\frac{1}{2}$–2 tablets of aspirin, depending on the animal's size, and foment the troublesome area with warm water infusions of fresh or dried comfrey leaf.

SMELLS

Old dogs may become somewhat odorous. The commonest source for a pong is the mouth. Check it for inflamed gums, loose teeth or encrustations of brownish plaque. If you've been paying attention to your pet's mouth hygiene throughout his life, such things should not arise. If they do, don't waste your cash on chlorophyll-containing deodorant tablets; pack Fido off to the vet, who can clean up the mouth and combat the inflammation and infection that produce smelly gases.

Other sources of smell in old animals are ears and bottoms. Look out for canker, particularly in breeds with floppy ears like spaniels. Where a dog is getting a trifle forgetful about how to pass a motion neatly and cleanly, see that his rear end is kept free of long hair that might get soiled and matted with stray faeces. Use the scissors round his anus if necessary.

A general deterioration in the coat of the OAP dog, with the production of more scurf and grease, may be the cause of 'old dog smell'. No problem: bath the venerable one every couple of weeks in a shampoo of the type made for humans and containing selenium.

BOWELS

In later years the bowels may become sluggish, unpredictable or loose. Make sure that you give plenty of bulk in the diet: fibrous vegetables, wholemeal bread, All-Bran etc should form an important part of the canine menu. Do not give much liver, and withhold bones. A teaspoon or two of Vi-Siblin granules sprinkled on the food every day or two can be a great help in forming healthy stools.

THE SENSES

The old dog naturally becomes a bit harder of hearing and dimmer of sight. A bluish-white appearance in the pupils of the eye is not necessarily a sign of cataracts. With age there is a change in the lens of the dog's eye, which may then reflect a small proportion of the light hitting it and thus make the normally invisible lens apparent to the human observer. Nevertheless the lens continues to let through the vast majority of the light which it receives. True old-age cataracts, opaque degenerations of the eye lens which are diagnosed by the veterinarian, usually develop slowly and are best left alone. I would not normally recommend surgery to remove the lenses in elderly animals. As the loss of sight comes on gradually, the dog has plenty of time to adjust to his familiar surroundings and with understanding on the part of his owner can get around perfectly well.

Nothing can usually be done about deafness although, together with some of the more general symptoms of senility, it can be markedly reduced in some cases by the use of drugs such as sulphapyrimidine and certain enzymes. These compounds are not suitable for certain animals; only your vet can decide whether or not to use them in any particular case.

EUTHANASIA

When the time comes, you may well be lucky enough to have your pet die quietly in his sleep. If not, as a responsible, loving owner you must be prepared to give him a dignified end by euthanasia at the proper time. Where an animal is in pain which cannot be easily relieved and is long-lasting, or where an animal is embarrassed, incapacitated or in any way precluded from leading a normal life to the extent that it is a nuisance to itself: these are the criteria by which you, in consultation with your vet, can decide when it is wise and right to decide upon euthanasia.

Euthanasia carried out by a qualified person is a peaceful, painless end. It is no more distressing than anaesthesia for a surgical operation. Avoid humane society clinics where animals are chloroformed or electrocuted. The best method is by overdosage of one of the anaesthetic chemicals, usually barbiturates, administered by your vet. The vet may inject the dog in one of a number of places – the animal will feel at most the prick of a hypodermic needle. Sometimes the animal passes away very quickly. Sometimes the dog will take some little time after losing consciousness before ceasing to breathe. Don't be alarmed; the drugs used by the vet are completely painless and once the animal is unconscious his pain and infirmities are blotted out forever by dreamless eternity. No, the vet will not recommend euthanasia by administering knock-out powders or pills. Although possible, this method is imprecise and long drawn out. He may, in the case of a very nervous or aggressive animal, provide you with a tranquilliser or sedative tablets to give to your pet beforehand, enabling the euthanasia injection proper to be given later to a quiet, possibly snoozing animal.

All the above applies equally to even the youngest puppy. Never ever drown an unwanted pup – or kitten, or any other animal. It is sheer cruelty.

7

There sprung a leak in Noah's ark,
Which made the Dog begin to bark;
Noah took his nose to stop the hole,
And hence his nose is always cold.
Children's rhyme, 1871

Breakdowns

The arts of medicine and surgery relating to the dog, be it a Cruft's champion or an RSPCA foundling, are now highly sophisticated veterinary specialities. The problems that can afflict the species are being intensively researched and much is known about both how similar and how different dogs are compared to other animals or to humans when unwell or in trouble.

An intricate machine needs a skilled mechanic. Do not tinker with your dog. My aim in this section of the book will be to explain symptoms, what you should do about them and simple, useful first-aid with an emphasis on the 'first'. Seek veterinary help for all but the mildest and briefest conditions. I will also outline the basic principles behind the commoner diseases of dogs, together with the ways in which the vet counter-attacks these afflictions.

But in all your pet's ailments, mild or serious, you will normally have to be prepared to do something, usually acting as nurse. There are some essential nursing techniques to be learned.

APPLYING A MAKESHIFT MUZZLE

This is essential where nervous, possessive, aggressive or sensitive (in pain) animals have to be handled or examined. Use a length of bandage, string, nylon stocking etc as illustrated. By carefully positioning the muzzle not too far

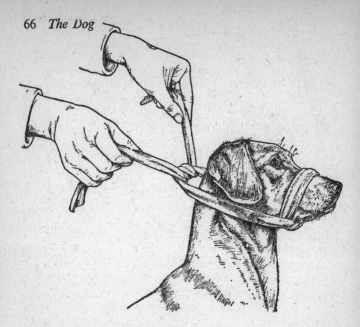

back, liquid medicine can be administered to such a dis-
armed dog by pouring it into the gap between the lips
behind the encircling band.

ADMINISTERING MEDICINE

Try to avoid putting medicines into food or drink: it can be
a very imprecise method. Tablets, pills or capsules should
be dropped into the V-groove at the back of the dog's
mouth while holding it open as illustrated, with one thumb
pressed firmly against the hard roof of the dog's mouth.

Liquids should be given slowly, a little at a time, by the
same method or into the lip pouch with the mouth held
closed: see diagram.

TAKING THE TEMPERATURE

You can't rely on the state of a dog's nose as an indicator of
temperature, good health or sickness. As with children,

being able to take your pet's temperature with a thermometer can help you to decide whether to call the doctor and can help him in diagnosing and treating what is wrong with the animal.

Use an ordinary glass thermometer bought from the chemist but preferably with a stubby rather than a slim bulb; better still, invest in an unbreakable thermometer, though these are more expensive. Lubricate it with a little Vaseline or olive oil and insert it for about one inch into the rectum. Once it is in place, hold the thermometer with the bulb angled against the rectal wall for good contact. After half a minute, remove the thermometer and read it.

A dog's normal temperature is 101·0–101·6°F. Allowing a slight rise for nervousness or excitement in some animals, you can expect under such conditions to read figures up to 101·8° or even 102·0°F. Higher than that is abnormal. Remember to shake down the mercury in the thermometer before use and to clean and disinfect the instrument afterwards.

GOING OUT OF TUNE

Like Alice I shall begin at the beginning and look at the mouth of the dog and then together we shall wander from head to tail through the various systems of the canine body.

The mouth

Commonest symptoms. Salivating (slavering), pawing at the mouth, exaggerated chewing motions, tentative chewing as if dealing with a hot potato, bad breath.

What you can do. This important sharp end of the animal should be inspected from time to time to see that all is in order. Cleaning of the teeth once or twice a week with cotton wool or a soft toothbrush dipped in salt water (or toothpaste from a tube kept specially for your pet) will stop the build-up of troublesome tartar. Giving chewable things like 'bones' and 'chews' made out of processed hide (available from the pet shop) and the occasional meal of coarse-cut, raw butcher's meat will also help. Providing bones of any kind does not keep tartar down.

When tartar, a yellowy-brown, cement-like substance, accumulates, it does not produce holes in the teeth that need filling. Instead it damages the gum edge, lets bacteria in to infect the tooth sockets and thus loosens the teeth. Tartar always causes some gum inflammation (gingivitis) and frequently bad breath.

If your pet displays the symptoms described, open his mouth and look for a foreign body stuck between his teeth. This may be a sliver of wood or bone stuck between two adjacent molars at the back of the mouth or, quite commonly, a bigger object jammed across the upper teeth against the hard palate. With patience, you can usually flick such foreign bodies out with a teaspoon handle or similar instrument.

Bright red edging to the gums where they meet the teeth, together with ready bleeding on gentle pressure, is a prime sign of gingivitis. Tap each tooth with your finger or a pencil. If there are any signs of looseness or tenderness, wash the mouth with warm water and salt, and give an aspirin tablet. There is little else you can do without professional help.

Canine dentistry is easily tackled by the vet. Using tranquillisers or short-acting general anaesthetics, he can remove tartar from teeth with special scrapers or the modern, ultra-sonic scaling machines. Bad teeth must be taken out to prevent root abscesses and socket infection from causing problems – septicaemia, simisitis or even kidney disease – elsewhere in the body.

Sometimes Fido breaks one of his teeth, perhaps by fighting or by chewing stones (a bad habit which some dogs get into). The large 'fang' teeth (canines) are most often the ones damaged. Surprisingly, these injuries do not usually produce signs of toothache, root infection or death of the tooth. Treatments used in human dentistry, like filling or crowning, are rarely necessary although perfectly possible. Their use has been limited to special cases such as alsatian

guard dogs, whose broken fangs have been repaired with acrylic or alloy materials.

Mouth ulcers, tumours (juvenile warts are common in young dogs) and tonsillitis need veterinary diagnosis and treatment where they are the cause of some of the symptoms listed above.

The eyes

Commonest symptoms. Sore, runny or mattery eyes. A blue or white film over the eye.

What you can do. If only one eye is involved and the only symptom is watering or sticky discharge without marked irritation, you can try washing the eye with warm Optrex or boracic acid powder in warm water every few hours, followed by the introduction of a little golden eye ointment onto the eyeball. There is an important technique in applying ointments to animal eyes: see diagram. Hold the tube parallel to the eyeball and pull the lower eyelid down slightly. Let a half-inch of ointment fall onto the eyeball or

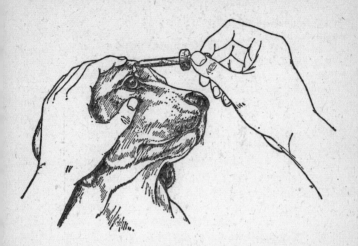

inside the lower lid. Now hold both lids closed for five seconds to allow the ointment to melt and begin dispersing.

Particularly in young dogs, *two* mattery eyes may indicate distemper. Persistent watering of one or both eyes can be due to very slight infolding (entropion) of the eyelid, or blocked tear ducts. A blue or white film over one or both eyes is normally a sign of keratitis (inflammation of the cornea); it is not a cataract but requires immediate veterinary attention. Opacity of the lens (cataract) is a blue or white 'film' much deeper in the eye. It usually occurs in older animals but may be seen in young pups (congenital cataract) and at other ages (diabetic cataract).

If any symptom in or around the eyes lasts for more than a day, take the patient to the vet.

Inflammations of the eye are treated by the vet in a variety of ways. He has antibiotic injections, drops and ointments available, other drugs to reduce inflammation and surgical methods of tackling ulcerated eyes under local anaesthesia. Problems due to infolding or deformed eyelids, foreign bodies embedded in the eyeball and even some cataracts can be treated surgically nowadays.

The nose

Commonest symptoms. Running, mattery nostrils. The appearance of having the human common cold. A cracked, sore, dry nose-tip. The dog 'with a cold', particularly if both eyes and nose are mattery, may well have distemper (see page 74).

What you can do. Don't let the nostrils get caked and clogged up. Bathe them thoroughly with warm water and anoint the nose pad with cold cream. If there is the 'common cold' symptom, seek veterinary advice at once. Old dogs with cracked, dry nose pads need regular attention to keep their nostrils free and to deal with bleeding from the cracks. Bathe the nose frequently, apply cod liver oil ointment twice or three times daily and work it well in, and give six drops of Abidec (from the chemists) or multivitamins as prescribed by the vet. The vet may use corticosteroid preparations on tough cases of sore noses.

The ears

Commonest symptoms. Shaking the head, scratching the ear. Pain on touching the ear, bad smell, discharge from the ear. Tilting the head to one side. Ballooning of the ear flap.

What you can do. Where symptoms suddenly appear, an effective emergency treatment is to pour copious quantities of warmed liquid paraffin into the ear (do this outside in the garden, for goodness sake). Acute inflammation will be greatly soothed by the oil. *Don't* stuff proprietary liquids into an ear; you don't know what you may be treating. Most of all, avoid so-called canker powders; the powder bases of these products can cause added irritation by forming annoying accumulations that act as foreign bodies.

See the vet early with ear trouble. Chronic ear complaints can be very difficult to eradicate.

Clean your dog's ears once a week. If it is a breed with hair growing in the ear canal (like a poodle or a Kerry blue) pluck the hair out between finger and thumb. Don't cut it. Using 'baby buds' or twists of cotton wool moistened in warm olive oil, clean the ear with a twisting action to remove excess brown ear wax.

Ear irritation may be due to various things which find their way into the ear canal. A grass awn may need professional removal. Small, barely visible white mange mites which live in dogs' ears cause itching and allow bacteria to set up secondary infections. Sweaty, dirty conditions, particularly in the badly ventilated ears of breeds such as the spaniel, provide an ideal opportunity for germs to multiply. The vet will decide whether mites, bacteria, fungi or other causes are the main source of inflammation, and will use antiparasitic, antibiotic or antifungal drugs as drops or injections. Where chronically inflamed ears are badly in need of drainage, sophisticated plastic surgery under general anaesthetic is often performed.

Although tilting of the head may be due simply to severe irritation on one side, it can indicate that the middle ear, the deeper part beyond the eardrum, is involved. Middle-ear disease does not necessarily result from outer-ear infection but may arise from trouble in the Eustachian tube that links the middle ear to the throat. It always needs rigorous veterinary attention with the use of antibiotics, antiflammatory drugs and, rarely, deep drainage operations.

The ballooning of an ear flap looks dramatic and serious but isn't. It is really a big blood blister, caused by the rupture of a blood vessel in the ear flap. It generally follows either vigorous scratching where ear irritation exists or a bite from another dog. It is treated surgically by the vet, who may drain it with a syringe or open it and then stitch the ear flap in a special way to prevent further trouble.

The chest

Commonest symptoms. Coughing, wheezing, laboured

breathing. Dogs can suffer from bronchitis, pleurisy, pneumonia, heart disease and other chest conditions. Coughing and sneezing, the signs of a 'head cold', possibly together with mattery eyes, diarrhoea and listlessness, may indicate the serious virus disease, distemper. Although commoner in younger animals, it can occur at any age and shows a variety of symptom combinations. Dogs catching distemper can and do recover, though the outlook is serious if there are symptoms such as fits, chorea (uncontrollable limb twitching) or paralysis, which suggest that the disease has affected the nervous system. These may not appear until many weeks after the virus first invades the body, and can be the only visible symptoms.

What you can do. Have your dog vaccinated against distemper at the first opportunity and keep the annual booster dose going.

At the first signs of generalised illness, like 'flu or a cold, contact the vet. Keep the animal warm, give him plenty of liquids and provide easily digestible nourishing food. If necessary, spoon in invalid food such as Complan, meat jelly, glucose and water. Give an aspirin, but don't waste time or money on patent 'cures'.

The vet, using clinical methods of examination, can confirm or deny the presence of distemper. Being caused by a virus, the disease is difficult to treat. Antibiotics and other drugs are used to suppress dangerous secondary bacterial infections. Vitamin injections strengthen the body's defences. The debilitating effects of coughing, diarrhoea and vomiting are countered by drugs which reduce these symptoms. Distemper antiserum, though available, is rarely useful as a cure; it is of value in protecting susceptible animals which have been in contact with the disease.

Other types of chest disease can be investigated by the vet using a stethoscope, X-rays, laboratory tests and electrocardiographs.

Where troublesome coughs occur in the older dog, give $\frac{1}{2}$–2 codeine tablets three times a day, depending on the animal's size, but see the vet. Heart disease is common in senior canine citizens and often responds well to treatment. Cheap drugs such as digitalis and theophylline can, under careful veterinary supervision, give a new lease of life to dogs with 'dicky' hearts.

It is useful in cases of heart trouble and indeed in all older dogs to give vitamin E in the synthetic form (50–200 mgms per day depending on the animal's size) or as wheat germ oil capsules (2–6 per day).

The stomach and intestines

Commonest symptoms. Vomiting, diarrhoea, constipation, blood in the droppings. There are numerous causes for any of these symptoms and sometimes more than one symptom will be observed at the same time. I shall only deal with the commonest symptoms and not attempt to describe all the diseases that can involve the abdominal organs. Any symptom persisting longer than twelve hours despite sensible first-aid treatment needs veterinary attention.

Vomiting may be simple and transient due to a mild infection (gastritis) of the stomach or to simple food poisoning. If severe, persistent or accompanied by other major signs, it can indicate the presence of serious conditions

such as distemper, contagious canine hepatitis, leptospirosis, heavy worm infestation or obstruction of the intestine.

Diarrhoea may be nothing more than the result of a surfeit of liver or a mild bowel infection. It may be more serious and profuse where important bacteria are present, in certain types of poisoning and in some allergies.

Constipation can be due to age, to a faulty diet including too much chomped-up bone or to obstruction.

Blood in the stools can arise from a variety of minor and major causes: from nothing more than a bone splinter scraping the rectal lining to the dangerous leptospiral infection.

What you can do. By all means try to alleviate the symptoms, but if they persist contact the vet no later than the following day.

With both vomiting and diarrhoea, it is important to replace liquids lost by the body. Cut out solid food, milk and fatty things. Give a little fluid – best of all glucose and water or weak bouillon cube broth – and often. Ice-cubes can be supplied for licking. Keep the animal warm and indoors. For vomiting administer 1–3 teaspoonsful of milk of magnesia, depending on the dog's size, every 3 hours. For diarrhoea give 2–8 teaspoonsful of Kaopectate (from the chemist) every 3 hours.

Don't use castor oil on constipated animals. Give instead liquid paraffin ($\frac{1}{2}$–2 tablespoonsful). Where an animal is otherwise well but you know it to be bunged up with something like bone which, after being crunched up, sets like cement in the bowels, get a Micralax enema from the chemist. This disposable, small, ready-loaded enema is very easy to use; just take off the top and insert the nozzle into the animal's rectum. Then squeeze, using half the contents for a toy breed and the full enema for all other sizes.

Abdominal conditions in general will need veterinary attention. Diseases such as contagious canine hepatitis and leptospirosis require intensive medical attack with antibiotics, transfusions to replace fluid, vitamins and minerals, and careful monitoring of progress by blood and urine tests.

Surgical techniques to remedy obstructions, foreign bodies and other tummy complaints are now highly sophisticated. Chloroform is a thing of the past and the vet and his team operate using modern anaesthetics such as halothane in theatres which are equipped with most of the paraphernalia of a human hospital.

Anal glands

Commonest symptoms. Two little glands, one on each side just within the anus, cause a lot of trouble for dogs. Owners complain of the animal rubbing its bottom along the floor or suddenly chasing its rear end as if stung by a bee. Worms are blamed as the cause; they rarely are. The anal glands are at the root of the problem, since they tend to become blocked up and impacted. By rubbing his bottom on the floor the dog will often clear the glands and relieve his

irritation. If the glands become infected, anal abscesses can result which may mean antibiotic therapy from the vet and, in chronic cases, surgical removal of the glands.

What you can do. Exercise the glands by ensuring that the dog produces bulky motions. Add fibrous foods such as vegetables to the diet. Mix a teaspoonful or two of Vi-Siblin or IsoGel granules to the meals once a day to give artificial bulk. Learn from the vet how to clean out the anal glands by squeezing them with a pad of cotton wool; see below.

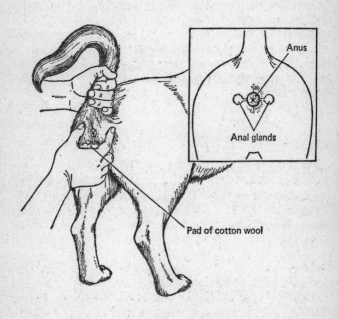

Anus

Anal glands

Pad of cotton wool

Urinary system

Commonest symptoms. Difficulty in passing urine, frequent urination, blood in urine.

What you can do. Although disease of the kidneys is a major area of canine medicine, it is outside the scope of owner treatment. Wherever and whenever you notice something wrong with the dog's waterworks, see the vet. Inflammation of the bladder (cystitis), stones in the bladder or associated tubes and kidney disease are common and need immediate professional advice. Whatever you do, don't withhold drinking water from an animal with urinary problems. Do remember to have your dog vaccinated against leptospirosis and visit the vet annually for a booster shot.

Cystitis, diagnosed early, responds well to treatment with antibiotics like ampicillin. A diagnosis of stones in the urinary system can be confirmed by X-ray and in most cases they are easily removed surgically.

Kidney disease needs careful management and supervision of diet. Chronic kidney disease patients can live to a ripe old age if the water, protein and mineral content of the diet are regulated, bacterial infection controlled, protein loss minimised and stress of any sort avoided.

Genitalia

Commonest symptoms. Although the male does develop genital problems from time to time (testicle tumours etc), the most important and common problems are found in the female: they include disorders of the heat period, persistent heat, heavy bleeding, and discharge of coloured matter from the vagina.

What you can do. Obviously any discharge in an animal known to be pregnant calls for immediate veterinary attention. In non-pregnant bitches the discharge, though looking like pus, is rarely caused by infection. It is usually a sign of pyometra, a hormonal womb inflammation. There is nothing you alone can do; see the vet at once. He may recommend medical treatment in the short term but eventually hysterectomy (removal of the womb surgically) will be advisable. This major operation, though serious, has a high success rate. To avoid such emergencies, have the bitch spayed as soon as you have decided you do not want any more puppies from her.

Mammary glands (breasts)

From time to time (say once a month), roll your bitch over and run your hands along her undercarriage. If you feel any hard lumps in the substance of the breast tissue, within the teats or just under the skin, see the vet at once. Breast tumours spread quickly to other parts of the body once established. Caught early they can be removed surgically.

Inflamed, hard breasts when a bitch is producing milk may indicate the onset of mastitis. This condition is commoner in breeds such as the boxer, particularly where there is a small litter or if the bitch loses her pups. The vet treats mastitis with antiflammatory and antibacterial drugs and sometimes will send the milk back by prescribing tablets of oestrogen.

The skin

There are many kinds of skin disease in dogs. Diagnosis needs examination and often sample analysis by the vet.

Commonest symptoms. Thin or bald patches in the coat; scratching; wet, dry or crusty sores. Mange, caused by an invisible mite, can cause crusty, hairless sores. Fleas, lice and ticks can cause damage to the coat. The presence of just one flea on a dog – terribly hard to track down – may set up widespread skin irritation as an allergic reaction to the flea's saliva injected when the little devil sucks. Dietary faults such as shortage of certain fats can produce a poor coat.

What you can do. If you see or suspect the presence of any of the skin parasites – mange mites, fleas, ticks or lice – obtain one of the antiparasitic aerosols, powders or baths from the pet shop, chemist or veterinary surgeon. Gammexane, bromocyclen ('Alugan') and dichlorvos ('Nuvan Top') preparations are among the most effective. Powders, however, are of little use against mange; drugs in bath or aerosol form are more appropriate. Tough, deep forms of mange such as demodectic mange may be treated by the vet using a combination of baths and drugs given by mouth. As there are several types of mange, let the vet advise on the best method of treating your particular case.

Ringworm, a subtle ailment, may need ultra-violet light examination or fungus culture from a hair specimen. Special drugs given by mouth or applied to the skin are needed for ringworm; care must be taken to see that human contacts don't pick up the disease from pets.

With all anti-parasite treatment of skin diseases, follow the instructions on the label of the preparation being used. With fleas, remember that the flea eggs are to be found not only on the animal's coat but also in his environment. Dog baskets, bedding, kennels etc must be sprayed with anti-parasite aerosol at the same time as the animal is treated.

Careful attention to providing a balanced diet will avoid most dietary skin disease. Sudden, sore, wet 'hot spots' that develop in summer or autumn may be caused by an allergy to plant pollen and other substances. Use scissors to clip the hair over and round the affected area to a level with the skin, and apply liquid paraffin liberally. Such cases will need veterinary attention, perhaps involving anti-histamine or corticosteroid creams, injections or tablets. Though dramatic, they are quickly settled by treatment.

Never apply creams, powders or ointments to skin disease without trimming back the hair. Don't encourage matting. Let oxygen get to the inflamed area.

Groom your pet regularly; it keeps the skin and coat healthy as well as tidy.

WORMS

Roundworms

These can cause unthriftiness and bowel upsets, particularly in puppies. They can spread to humans and occasionally damage babies severely.

Rid your dog of roundworms by giving one of the modern worming drugs (piperazine, mebendazole, dichlorvos etc) at regular three-month intervals throughout his life.

Tapeworms

These worms do not usually cause much trouble to dogs but can spread to humans occasionally. They have a life cycle passing through fleas.

Keep your dog free of fleas. Tapeworm segments look like grains of boiled rice or off-white bits of flat tape up to one centimetre long and may move a little. If you see them in the stools or stuck to the hair round the anus, give the dog a dose of one of the modern tapeworm drugs such as bunamidine or niclosamide. These can be obtained from the vet. One drug, mebendazole, kills roundworms and tapeworms in the dog.

BITES AND WOUNDS

As soon as you detect a bite or wound, clip the hair around its edges down to the skin with scissors. Bathe the area thoroughly in a strong solution of epsom salts in warm water. Apply antiseptic cream, *not* powder, to any small injury that is not likely to need professional attention. Where a bite is involved, a single, long-acting shot of penicillin from the vet is a prudent measure. Minor wounds are best left without any dressing; exposure to the oxygen of the air is beneficial.

Cut paw pads are troublesome but not serious. They heal slowly and are usually not stitchable. Cover the paw with a child's cotton sock after cleaning it and applying antiseptic ointment. Do *not* tie on a waterproof dressing such as a plastic bag. Never fix a foot dressing with a rubber band. The dressing must allow air through and should be held by a strip of adhesive tape or a few turns of narrow bandage.

Sadly, dog fights as a source of human entertainment didn't die out with the nineteenth century. There has been a resurgence of this 'sport' in recent years, particularly in Canada, the USA and Mexico. It is promoted by underground magazines – one is called 'Pit Dogs' – which give form, tips and round-by-round descriptions of recent contests for the aficionados. The American Dog Owners' Association reckons that over a thousand such contests are held annually in the United States and that the disgusting 'sport' is growing.

ACCIDENTS

First, get the patient away from further danger and into a quiet, warm place indoors. Slip a sheet underneath him and carry him as in a hammock or, if possible, by the scruff of the neck. Do not waste time or stand on ceremony. Shock is your principal adversary. Lay him comfortably on a warm blanket. Place a hot (not scalding) water bottle next to him. Do not give alcoholic stimulants. Do not give aspirin. You may try to spoon in a few teaspoonsful of warm, sweet tea. If something is bleeding badly, slap a thick pad of cotton wool or lint or a folded handkerchief onto the place and press firmly – if necessary until the vet arrives. Do not try splinting limbs or experimenting with tourniquets.

Remember that it saves time to be doing all this in a car on the way to the vet's surgery, rather than waiting for the vet to come to you.

There are many other areas of canine medicine on which it is not appropriate to touch in a little volume such as this. I should perhaps only repeat what I said earlier: don't tinker with this marvellous and valuable machine. If your pet isn't running well, take him straight along to see his GP.

To own a dog, after all, isn't just a great pleasure, it is also a great privilege. Look after it and it will do much for you: as Alexander Pope said in a letter to a friend in 1709,

'Histories are more full of examples of the fidelity of dogs than of friends.'

Index

Also available in this series

THE CAT

David Taylor is a well-known veterinary surgeon and the author of three books about his work as a wildlife vet: *Zoovet, Doctor in the Zoo* and *Going Wild*. He has also been a regular guest on BBC television's *Animal Magic* where he has advised on less exotic animals – the family pet. *The Cat*, one of a series of practical books by David Taylor, gives specialist, helpful and humorous advice on living with and caring for your cat. Everything the cat lover needs to know is presented in this book with the aid of diagrams and some light-hearted cartoons.

In preparation

THE PONY
THE SMALL PET
THE CAGE BIRD
THE EXOTIC PET